APR 2 3 2019

W9-AVR-508

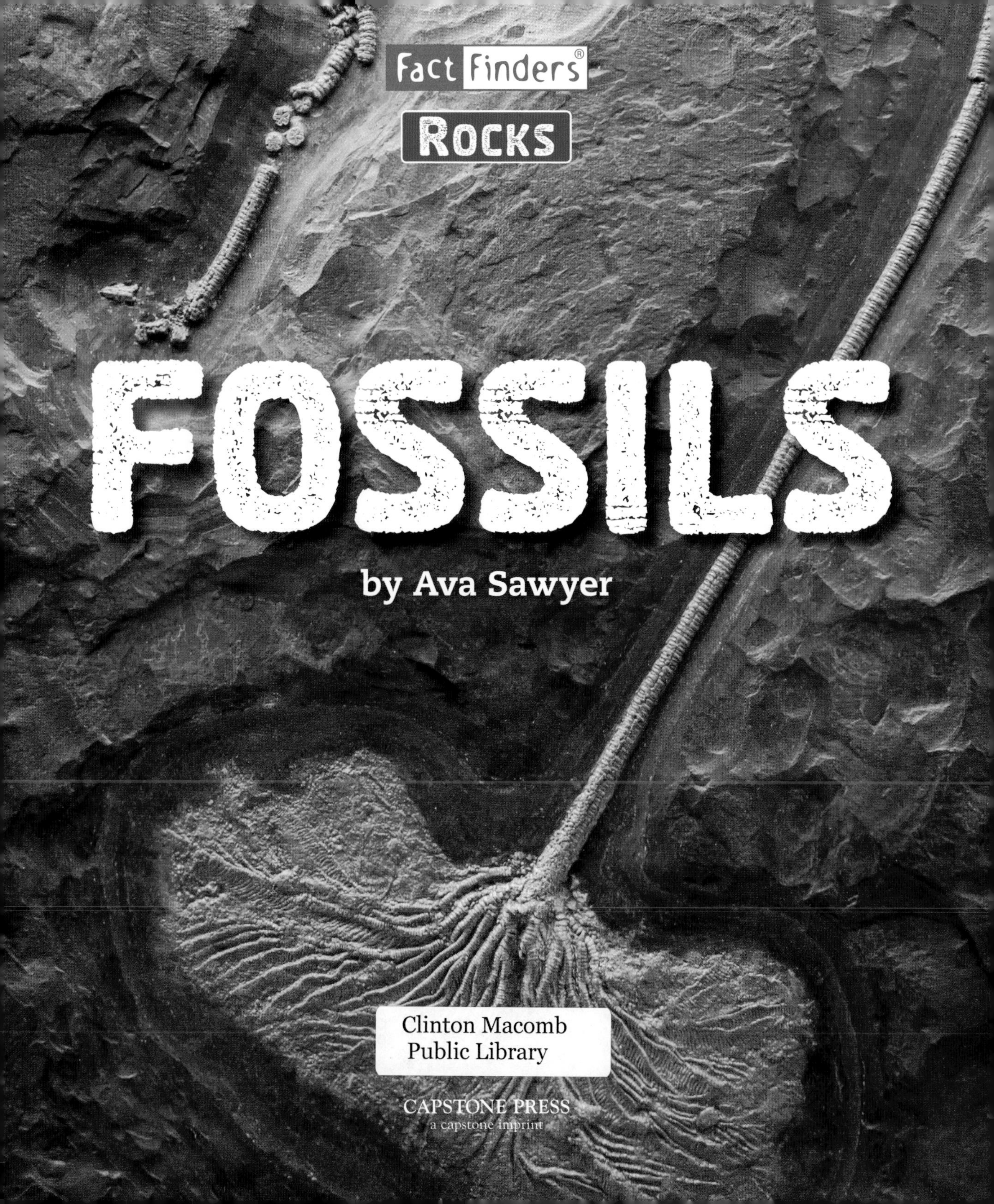

Fact Finders®

Rocks

FOSSILS

by Ava Sawyer

Clinton Macomb
Public Library

CAPSTONE PRESS
a capstone imprint

Fact Finders Books are published by Capstone Press,
1710 Roe Crest Drive, North Mankato, Minnesota 56003
www.mycapstone.com

Library of Congress Cataloging-in-Publication Data
Names: Sawyer, Ava, author.
Title: Fossils / by Ava Sawyer.
Description: North Mankato, Minnesota : Capstone Press, [2018] |
Series: Fact finders. Rocks | "Fact Finders is published by Capstone
    Press." | Audience: Ages 8–10. | Includes index.
Identifiers: LCCN 2017059332 (print) | LCCN 2017061656 (ebook)
    | ISBN 9781543527162 (ebook PDF) | ISBN 9781543527001
    (library binding) | ISBN 9781543527087 (paperback)
Subjects: LCSH: Fossils—Juvenile literature.
Classification: LCC QE714.5 (ebook) | LCC QE714.5 .S29 2018
    (print) | DDC 560—dc23
LC record available at https://lccn.loc.gov/2017059332

Editorial Credits
Editor: Nikki Potts
Designer: Sarah Bennett
Media Researcher: Jo Miller
Production Specialist: Laura Manthe

Image Credits
Alamy: Anne Heine, 11; Newscom: imageBROKER/Fabian von
Poser, 17; Science Source: elxeneize, 29, Gary Hincks, 9 (all),
Pascal Goetgheluck, 15, Phil Degginger, 28, SPL, 13; Shutterstock:
AKKHARAT JARUSILAWONG, 27, (top), alice-photo, 4, alinabel,
19, Bjoern Wylezich, 10 (top), Cristina Nixau, 12-13, Designua, 7
(both), Dinoton, 25, Dorothy Chiron, 18, Galyna Andrushko, 24-25,
I love photo, 23 (middle top), Linda Bucklin, 27 (bottom), Linnas,
23 (middle bottom),Lippert Photography, 6, Mark Godden, 20,
Martin Kemp, 2-3, Miroslav Halama, cover, Nadezda Murmakova,
24 (right), paleontologist natural, 1, 5, Patryk Kosmider, 23
(bottom), Paula Karu, 24 (left), ribeiroantonio, 8, Romans_1_20,
10 (bottom), ruiztome, 22, W. Scott McGill, 16, YuRi Photolife, 23
(top); Wikimedia: Dallas Krentzel, 26, Mitternacht90, 21, Wellcome
Images, 14

Design Elements
Shutterstock: Budimir Jevtic

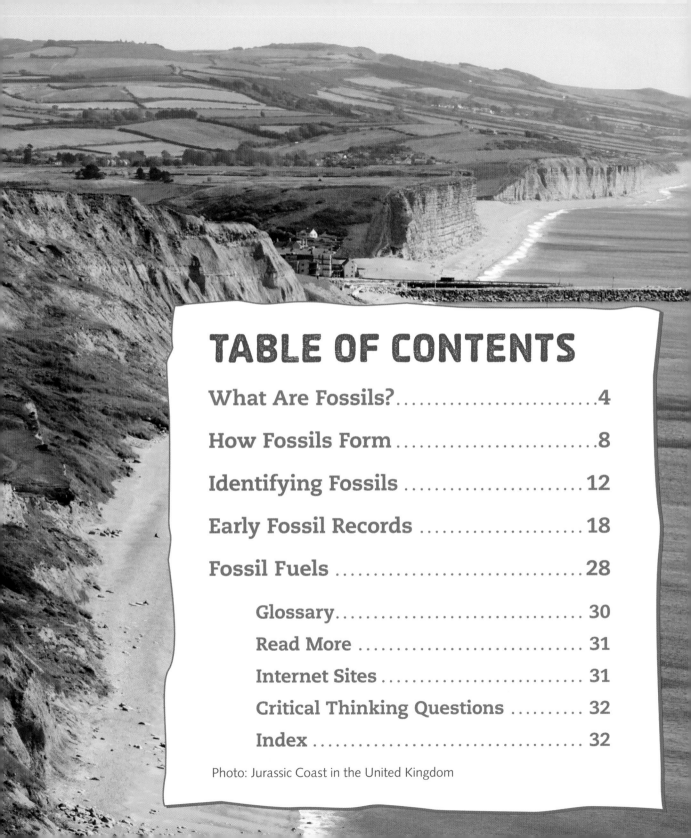

TABLE OF CONTENTS

Photo: Jurassic Coast in the United Kingdom

CHAPTER 1

WHAT ARE FOSSILS?

The remains of a tyrannosaurus rex are found in western United States. **Paleontologists** carefully brush away the surrounding dust and rock to remove the bones. Across the world, a nearly perfect imprint of a plant leaf is found in a rock in central India. For most of Earth's long history, there were no written records. These fossils provide very important clues to our planet's past.

Fossils are the remains or impressions of plants and animals. These organisms did not live yesterday, last year, or even hundreds of years ago. It takes millions of years for a fossil to form.

FACT

The science of fossils is called **paleontology**. A scientist who studies fossils is called a paleontologist.

---

paleontologist—scientist who studies fossils

4   paleontology—the science that deals with fossils and other ancient life-forms

A paleontologist uses a brush to carefully expose a dinosaur fossil found in sedimentary rock.

5

Fossils have been found on every continent on Earth. These fossils provide clues about what life was like on Earth millions of years ago. For example, the fossils that have been found at the South Pole are from tropical plants and animals. Scientists think those fossils show that the landmass at the South Pole, which is now icy and cold, used to have a hot, wet climate. That means the landmasses of Earth have moved over time. The fossils show that long ago, the continent of Antarctica must have been closer to the equator. In other places on Earth, fossils show that the land was once covered by water. Scientists have found fossils of fish, sharks, and sea plants in desert areas. Because these organisms would not have lived in a desert environment, a large body of water must have once covered the land.

PANGAEA

In 1912, a German scientist named Alfred Wegener proposed an idea known as the plate tectonic theory. He noticed that Earth's continents seemed to fit together like a puzzle. He proposed the idea that the continents were once all part of one giant landmass called Pangaea, meaning "many lands." He believed that over time, the continents drifted apart into their current locations.

There are a few major pieces of evidence that support the theory of plate tectonics. First, the continents look like they once fit together. Take South America and Africa, for example. If you take away the Atlantic Ocean and squeeze these two continents together, they fit like a glove.

Second, the same types of rocks and fossils are found on continents that are oceans apart. For example, fossils of the fern *Glossopteris* are found in South America, Africa, India, Antarctica, and Australia.

Third, there is evidence of places on Earth that once had a different climate. One example of evidence is coal, an organic material created from the remains of plants. Antarctica is a frozen wasteland now with very few plants growing on it. The presence of coal in Antarctica reveals that this icy continent was once in a much warmer area.

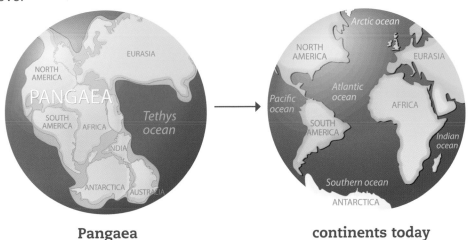

Pangaea   **continents today**

7

CHAPTER 2

How Fossils Form

Long ago, our world was very different. Life was only present in the oceans, and no animals or plants lived on land. Therefore, most fossils were formed under the sea. An **ammonite** is a good example of how fossils can form. The ammonite was a sea animal that had a spiral shell. It took hundreds of thousands or even millions of years for an ammonite shell to turn into a fossil.

First, the ammonite died and sank to the seabed. The soft parts of its body, such as muscles and skin, rotted away. The hard part of the body—the shell—was left behind. Layers of sand and sediment then buried the shell. Water flowed through the shell over time. The minerals carried by the water replaced the minerals in the shell.

ammonite

As more layers of sediment piled up, more pressure was added to the shell. This pressure caused the sediment to form into sedimentary rock. At the same time, the new minerals in the shell hardened into a rock that was the same shape as the original shell. Finally, a fossil that looked like the shell formed. It was buried deep in the sedimentary rock, just waiting to be discovered.

FACT

Fossils are often found as molds or shapes in rock. When an animal or a shell dissolves away, it leaves a mold of itself in the rock. Sometimes a mold becomes filled with minerals. The minerals take the shape of the mold. This is called a cast.

FOSSIL FORMATION

1. The process begins when the dinosaur or other animal dies and the body ends up in a location where fossilization is possible, such as in sediments below water.

2. The soft tissues decay, while minerals in the dinosaur's skeleton are gradually replaced by minerals from the mud. These minerals solidify into a form of stone or rock, preserving the shape and structure of the skeleton.

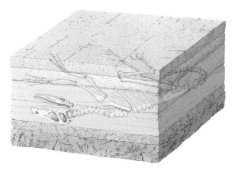

3. The fossil may remain underground or may eventually be exposed by erosion of the surrounding material.

ammonite—a sea animal that had a spiral shell

9

Not all fossils are found in rocks. Some are found in ice. Others are found in sticky substances such as amber and tar.

In some cold parts of the world, the ground is frozen year round. Animals became frozen in this ice. They became perfect fossils.

Amber is a yellow-orange material. It began as a runny, sticky fluid. The fluid came from ancient pine trees. Millions of years ago, insects became stuck in it. The amber hardened around them to produce fossils.

amber fossil

Tar is a thick, sticky substance. Tar pits are large pools of tar. In ancient times, animals sometimes became stuck in tar pits. They died there and became fossils.

BURGESS SHALE

Fossils containing the soft parts of animals and plants are very rare. However, lots of soft-bodied fossils have been found in the Burgess shale. This is a layer of rocks found in an area of the Rocky Mountains in British Columbia, Canada.

About 500 million years ago, the area was buried in moving mud. Animals were trapped in the mud. The mud hardened to form the rock shale. There was no time for the animals' soft parts to rot away. The plants and animals became soft-bodied fossils.

Visitors explore a Burgess shale fossil site at Yoho National Park in British Columbia, Canada.

CHAPTER 3

IDENTIFYING FOSSILS

Once a fossil is found, how do scientists know what kind of plant or animal it used to be? This question is especially important because many fossils are of **extinct organisms**.

The first thing scientists do is compare the fossil to other fossils that have been found. If scientists determine that a fossil is from a new organism, they get to name it. In 2009, a scientist found a fossil of a **primate**. He named it Ida after his 5-year-old daughter.

extinct—no longer living; an extinct animal is one that has died out, with no more of its kind

organism—a living plant or animal

primate—any animal in the group of mammals that includes humans, apes, and monkeys; primates use their fingers and thumbs to hold objects

Jurassic Coast in the United Kingdom

MARY ANNING

Mary Anning (1799–1847) was born in Lyme Regis located on the southern coast of England. Her father was a cabinetmaker and an avid fossil hunter. Mary became a fossil hunter at a young age after her father died. She hoped to earn money from selling fossils. She would rush out after storms that caused land to slide away and expose new fossils. Mary sold hundreds of fossils. The well-known tongue-twister "She sells seashells by the seashore" was inspired by Mary Anning.

Many credit Mary for discovering the first ichthyosaurus fossil. She also discovered the first plesiosaur. Due to lack of proper documentation and because she was female, Mary was not given credit for many of her discoveries.

Mary Anning

13

Scientists also have to verify that what they find are real fossils. The discoveries could be fakes made to trick the scientific community. For example, a fossil found in 1912 had both human and orangutan characteristics. Many people thought it was an exciting scientific find and continued to think so for the next 41 years. However, in 1953, a team of scientists discovered that it was actually an orangutan's jaw glued to a human skull. Today, scientists use X-ray machines to make sure that fossils are real. When they look at images from X-rays, scientists are able to see where pieces may have been forcefully joined together.

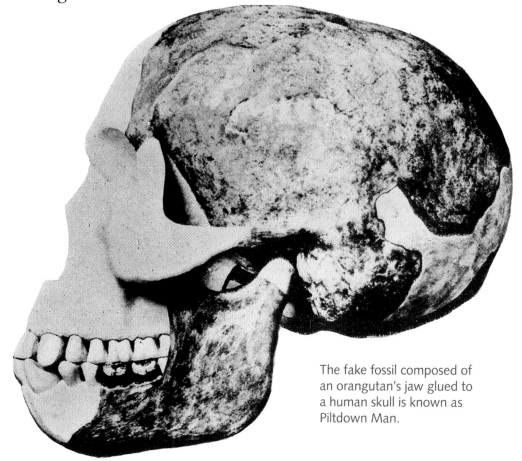

The fake fossil composed of an orangutan's jaw glued to a human skull is known as Piltdown Man.

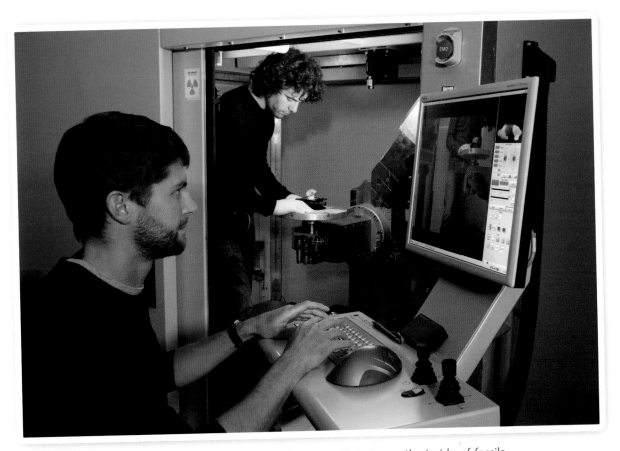
High-resolution X-ray scanning allows scientists to see the inside of fossils.

Another step in the identification process is to determine the age of fossils. One way of doing this is by a process called radiometric dating. This process looks at certain **elements** in the fossil. Some types of elements change to another element over time. This is called radioactive decay. Scientists can look at how much of certain types of elements are in the fossil. They use this information to determine the age of the fossil. Uranium, potassium, rubidium, and carbon are some of the elements that can be used for determining the age of objects.

element—a substance made of atoms that cannot be broken down into simpler substances

15

TYPES OF FOSSILS

Fossils are divided into two groups. Some fossils are just part of an organism, such as a bone, a shell, or a tooth. Some fossils are complete organisms. For example, fully fossilized trees and dinosaurs have been found. These types of fossils are called body fossils. **Petrified** trees and leaf imprints are also body fossils. These fossils show us what life was like millions of years ago.

Fossils are not always the actual remains of plants and animals. Trace fossils are traces that prehistoric animals left behind, such as footprints, eggs, droppings, plant seeds, and burrows. Trace fossils tell us something about how ancient creatures lived—how they moved, what they ate, and how they raised their young. For example, dinosaur tracks have been found in many places in southern Utah. Paleontologists are able to use tracks to tell how big the dinosaur was and how fast it could run.

coprolite

FACT

Ancient droppings are called **coprolites**. Some coprolites contain shells or bones. Some contain fish scales. Coprolites help scientists learn what ancient animals ate.

petrified—a material that has been changed into stone or a stony substance by water and minerals

coprolite—a fossilized animal dropping

16

fossilized footprints
of a tyrannosaurus rex
in Cameroon, Africa

17

CHAPTER 4

EARLY FOSSIL RECORDS

Fossils provide many clues about Earth's history. There are no written records that tell all of the details about Earth's origins. We have to look at what was left behind and draw conclusions from that information. Fossils are a great way to learn more about Earth's history. They tell us how Earth's crust and climate have changed over time. They also tell us what kinds of plants and animals used to live on Earth. Together, this information is called the fossil record.

Scientists think the first living things that became fossils were **cyanobacteria**. Layers of these blue-green bacteria built up into rocks called stromatolites. Most of these fossils are found in the oceans or along the coastlines of the continents. Scientists estimate that those fossils formed at least 3.5 billion years ago.

Stromatolites are found in the World Heritage Area of Shark Bay, Western Australia.

18   cyanobacteria—blue-green algae

GEOLOGIC TIMESCALE

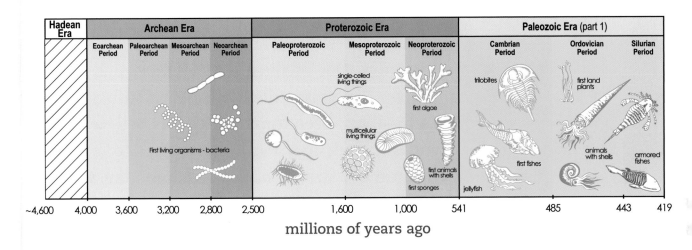

millions of years ago

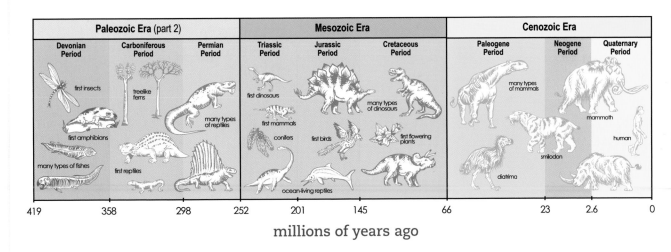

millions of years ago

GEOLOGIC TIMESCALE

Scientists have used information from fossils to divide up the history of Earth. This is called the geologic timescale. It is divided into stages called eras. Each era is made up of shorter stages called periods.

19

The first animals to become fossils lived in the sea. They had soft bodies and no backbones or vertebrae. These invertebrates, which include sponges, jellyfish, and sea worms, were fossilized about 600 million years ago. Later, some invertebrates developed shells for protection. One of the most well known is the spiral-shelled ammonite. The ammonite is the oldest animal with a shell for which a fossil has been found. Scientists believe this animal lived 415 million years ago.

Ammonites grew to enormous sizes. The largest ammonite fossil was 5 feet (1.5 meters) across. Although they lived in the oceans, scientists have actually found some ammonite fossils on top of the Himalayas—the tallest mountains on Earth. The land that makes up those mountains was once at the bottom of an ocean.

An ammonite fossil is found in a sedimentary rock located on the Jurassic Coast in the United Kingdom.

dunkleosteus skull fossil

The first fish in the sea lived about 450 million years ago. They were worm-like creatures that sucked food from the seabed. Later there were bony fish with jaws and teeth. The dunkleosteus lived nearly 380 million years ago. Fossils show that this monster was 32 feet (10 m) long, and its jagged, bony jaws gave it the strongest bite of any fish that ever lived.

21

PLANT AND JUNGLE FOSSILS

Fossils provide evidence that plants began to live on Earth about 400 million years ago. By 300 million years ago, Earth had a hot, tropical climate. Just like plants in tropical rain forests today, plants in prehistoric times grew quickly and often to enormous sizes. The hot, wet conditions provided the right environment for plants to grow. Some of the prehistoric jungle ferns were nearly 50 feet (15 m) tall. Other plants that today are tiny mosses were about 130 feet (40 m) tall in prehistoric times.

plant fossil

Tropical rain forests of today do not just contain plant life. Animals live there as well. This was also the case with the prehistoric jungles. Insects such as beetles and flies lived there. There were also millipedes 6 feet (2 m) long scuttling along the forest floor and giant dragonflies flying in the air. We know all of this information about the prehistoric jungles because of the fossils that were left behind.

trilobite

beetle

dragonfly

AMPHIBIAN AND REPTILE FOSSILS

One of the earliest land animals was the ichthyostega. The "ichthy" prefix means that these animals had fishlike qualities. They had heads and tails similar to fish, but they also had legs that allowed them to walk on land. Today, animals such as amphibians can survive on land and in water. They must live near the water to keep their skin moist. Their bodies are slippery and wet like fish. They also lay their eggs in the water environment. However, they live on dry land.

lizard

frog

160 million-year-old crocodile fossil

Reptiles were also some of the earliest land animals. Just as the plants and fish grew to huge sizes, so did the reptiles. One snake fossil found was 42 feet (13 m) long and weighed 2,500 pounds (1,134 kilograms), which is longer than a bus and heavier than a car. The biggest crocodile was 50 feet (15 m) long.

25

A tyrannosaurus rex fossil stands in the Field Museum in Chicago, Illinois.

DINOSAURS

The most commonly known super-sized prehistoric reptiles are the dinosaurs. These animals included hundreds of varieties. They lived in the sea and on land. Fossil records show these animals lived on Earth for about 165 million years, during the Mesozoic Era (250 million to 65 million years ago).

Scientists use fossils to show relationships between different animals and how animals **evolve**, or change over time. Perhaps one of the most amazing examples of evolution is that of birds. Birds are actually living dinosaurs, the one surviving group of creatures that otherwise went extinct 65 million years ago.

FACT

Nobody knows exactly why all the dinosaurs died out around 65 million years ago. Most scientists believe they were wiped out when a huge asteroid hit Earth.

evolve—when something develops over a long time with gradual changes

26

Birds evolved from a group of dinosaurs called theropods. They were creatures that walked on their hind legs and mostly ate meat. Scientists discovered that many theropods had feathers. While most dinosaurs could not fly, the feathers still would have been useful. Feathers trap warm air close to the body and could have kept hatchling dinosaurs warm. Also, while most dinosaurs could not achieve true flight, some did glide.

Because of new fossil discoveries, scientists have learned the birdlike dinosaur, the archaeopteryx, had feathers from head to toe. Prior to the fossil discovery, the bird was thought to only have had feathers on its wings and tail.

archaeopteryx

CHAPTER 5

FOSSIL FUELS

Besides providing information about Earth's history, fossils help us in another way—by providing an energy source. **Fossil fuels** are formed from ancient plants and animals. For example, coal comes from ancient plants. The plants sank into the mud. Then they were covered with layers and layers of mud that eventually formed into rock. The plant remains were crushed under all of that pressure. Heat and pressure inside Earth changed the remains to black coal. Coal can be burned to produce heat and energy.

Coal is exposed on the coast in Nova Scotia, Canada.

Other examples of fossil fuels include oil and gas. Oil and gas are the remains of billions of microscopic marine animals and plants that were buried in mud on the seabed. The remains continued to be buried deeper and deeper. As the mud turned to rock, the animal and plant remains slowly turned to oil and gas, trapped in layers of rock. Humans drill down into the rock to get the oil and gas out.

Even though fossil fuels are helpful for people, they are harmful to the environment. When fossil fuels are burned, they release gases such as carbon dioxide into the air. These gases cover Earth like a blanket, trapping the heat inside. Many scientists think these gases have contributed to the increased warming of Earth.

To help lessen the negative impact on the environment, humans are turning to alternative energy sources. Wind, water, solar, and geothermal are alternative energy forms that create less pollution. These sources of energy are renewable, which means they will not run out.

Wind turbines and solar panels collect renewable energy.

fossil fuel—a natural fuel formed from the remains of plants and animals; coal, oil, and natural gas are fossil fuels

geothermal—relating to the intense heat inside Earth

29

GLOSSARY

coprolite (KAH-pruh-lyt)—a fossilized animal dropping

cyanobacteria (sye-uh-noh-bak-TEER-ee-uh)—blue-green algae

element (EL-uh-muhnt)—a substance made of atoms that cannot be broken down into simpler substances

evolve (i-VAHLV)—when something develops over a long time with gradual changes

extinct (ik-STINGKT)—no longer living; an extinct animal is one that has died out, with no more of its kind

fossil fuel (FAH-suhl FYOOL)—a natural fuel formed from the remains of plants and animals; coal, oil, and natural gas are fossil fuels

geothermal (jee-oh-THUR-muhl)—relating to the intense heat inside Earth

organism (OR-guh-niz-uhm)—a living plant or animal

paleontologist (pale-ee-uhn-TOL-uh-jist)—scientist who studies fossils

paleontology (pale-ee-uhn-TOL-uh-jee)—the science that deals with fossils and other ancient life-forms

petrified (PET-ruh-fide)—a material that has been changed into stone or a stony substance by water and minerals

primate (PRYE-mate)—any animal in the group of mammals that includes humans, apes, and monkeys; primates use their fingers and thumbs to hold objects

READ MORE

Oxlade, Chris. *Fossils*. Rock On! Chicago: Heinemann Raintree, 2016.

Snedden, Robert. *Mary Anning, Fossil Hunter*. Superheros of Science. New York: Gareth Stevens, 2016.

VanVoorst, Jenny Fretland. *Fossils*. Rocks and Minerals. Minneapolis: Abdo Publishing, 2015.

INTERNET SITES

Use FactHound to find Internet sites related to this book.

Visit *www.facthound.com*

Just type in 9781543527001 and go.

 Check out projects, games and lots more at
www.capstonekids.com

CRITICAL THINKING QUESTIONS

1. What are the two types of fossils? Define each type.

2. What is the plate tectonic theory?

3. How are body fossils formed?

INDEX